UNTIL YOU'RE THE PASTOR...
YOU'RE NOT

PASTOR STAMFORD B. JACKSON SR.

Table of Contents

Table of Contents

Foreword
First Lady Michelle Warren

There are some words that don't fade with time they grow louder, richer, and more meaningful as the years go by. My late husband, Apostle K. L. Warren, had a way of speaking wisdom that stayed with you long after the conversation ended. One of his most memorable sayings was:

"Until you're the Pastor, you're NOT!"

He said it often, especially to those eager to do great things in ministry. At first, people would laugh or nod some even got angry not fully grasping what he meant. But as they grew in the things of God, those words began to unfold with revelation.

Apostle K. L. Warren wasn't trying to discourage anyone; he was teaching a vital truth that shepherding God's people is not about position, but preparation. It's not about having a title, but about being trusted by God with His people.

He understood that before a person can lead, they must first learn to serve. Before God can elevate, He must first develop. Pastoring isn't something you decide to do it's something God calls and qualifies you for. My husband carried that revelation with humility and grace. He loved deeply, corrected firmly, and led faithfully. His strength as a leader flowed from his heart as a servant.

Many who served under him admired his anointing, but few understood the cost behind it—the nights of prayer, the burdens he carried, the patience required to truly shepherd souls. He often reminded his leaders that it takes more than charisma to care for God's people—it takes character, compassion, and consistency.

As I read this book, written by our son, Stamford Jackson, my heart is full. I see his father's spirit reflected in his words—the same depth, wisdom, and love for God's church. This book doesn't just carry a title; it carries a truth that shaped our ministry and continues to shape lives today.

My prayer is that as you read *Until You're the Pastor, You're NOT!* you will hear Apostle K. L. Warren's voice as clearly as I still do—teaching, challenging, and encouraging with that blend of humor, firmness, and love that made him who he was. His legacy lives on through every lesson he taught, every life he touched, and now, through these pages.

May his words continue to inspire a new generation to embrace the process, honor the calling, and trust God's timing.

— First Lady Michelle Warren

Co-Founder, Hebron Cornerstone Church International

Tampa, Florida

Foreword
By Pastor Charles McCarley

"*Either you're called, or you're crazy.*"

That's a phrase I've often heard throughout my journey. And truthfully, I believe I am both because who would willingly choose to be in such a position? The position we have come to know as a *joyous burden.*

The office of the pastor is often surrounded by admiration and perceived glamour, but few truly see the private burdens leaders carry within their homes, their ministries, and upon their families. It is imperative that those who feel the pull toward ministry understand that it is not always applause and celebration. In this walk, you will experience stressful, challenging, hurtful, and even betraying moments.

Yet, there will be no greater joy than witnessing those whom God has entrusted to your care walk in spiritual maturity and divine purpose. Beloved, we are the faceless representation of the handiwork of the Spirit of God not for our glory, but for His. They should not see us; they should see Him.

It is in those sacred moments that we come to understand the depth of this phrase, *joyous burden*. Yes, the weight of ministry will always be present, but Scripture reminds us:

"Greater is He that is in you, than he that is in the world."

1 John 4:4

William Shakespeare once wrote:

"Be not afraid of greatness. Some are born great, some achieve greatness, and some have greatness thrust upon them."

Many of us can relate to this truth. Ministry is not always our first choice. I, too, can testify to not wanting to be called to the pastorate. Yet, when you completely surrender your life to Christ, you soon learn that certain permissions are no longer yours to give. The Spirit of the Lord will assign you to tasks you did not request because greatness is thrust upon you, not to break you, but because the Master has need of you.

When our beloved Founder, Pastor Deborah Scott, completed her earthly journey and was called home to eternal glory, there was only one person she desired to continue her work in the earth. I did not seek it, but it was thrust upon me, and the Lord has been faithful ever since.

My prayer is that as you read this book, you will hear a clear message to every leader: this call to ministry is sacred, serious, and of the utmost importance. Many have folded under pressure, but you must stand your ground and be ready in season and out of season.

Let this book encourage you and remind you that you are not alone on this journey. It is easy to criticize and easy to complain, but until you sit in the seat of a pastor you are not the pastor.

So know who you are and walk boldly therein. Learn from these pages, prayerfully and transparently crafted, to pull back the curtain on what it truly means when God calls you to walk at this level of surrender.

May these words guide and comfort you. And always remember I am praying for you, that you might become the kind of leader who shifts atmospheres and changes worlds.

Go be great!

Because of Christ,

Pastor Charles McCarley

Senior Servant, Tabernacle of Praise Buffalo

Fusion Fellowship of Churches

Preface
By Dr. Annetta M. Williams-Jackson

There are moments in life when destiny and preparation collide, and it becomes evident that the hand of God has been guiding all along. *Until You're the Pastor… You're Not!* Is more than a book it is a testimony of process, perseverance, and purpose.

I have watched my husband, Pastor Stamford B. Jackson Sr., walk through storms, trials, and valleys. Each test seemed designed to break him, yet God used them to build him. Every disappointment became a classroom, every battle a training ground, and every season of waiting a holy refining fire. Through it all, God preserved him. He was kept when others counted him out. He was elevated when others overlooked him. He was prepared in private so he could be promoted in the Kingdom.

This book does not merely speak to a title or position it speaks to the weight of calling, the responsibility of shepherding, and the journey of becoming. You do not become a pastor by desire alone; you become a pastor when the oil of God, tested through trials and affirmed through perseverance, rests upon your life. You are not the pastor until you have carried the cross before the crown until you have walked with God in the shadows before He reveals you in the light.

When you asked me to serve as Co-Pastor, my thought was simple: *"I'm already supportive without the title, so let's get it done."* Because ministry is not about recognition, but responsibility not about status, but service. I had already been walking beside you in prayer, sacrifice, and vision. The title only confirmed what God had already written on our hearts.

For every reader, may these words remind you that your process has purpose. God does not waste pain, nor does He ignore faithfulness. What He preserves, He promotes. What He anoints, He appoints. And just as He has done in the life of Pastor Jackson, He will do in yours.

As you turn these pages, prepare your heart. You will not just read about leadership you will encounter the God who raises leaders. You will see how storms shape strength, how endurance births authority, and how true pastoral ministry is less about a title and more about a life laid down.

This is not just his story. It is a Kingdom blueprint. May it stir every leader, every servant, and every believer to trust the God who calls, keeps, and completes His work in us.

Dr. Annetta M. Williams-Jackson

Psychology, Philosophy & Biblical Counseling

Kingdom Vision Center International Ministries

Fort Worth, Texas

Dedication

This work is dedicated first and foremost to **God**, the Author and Finisher of my faith, whose calling, grace, and sustaining power made this journey possible.

It is also dedicated to my **beautiful and amazing wife**. Thank you for your unwavering support, your constant encouragement, and your loving push to stay the course when the road grew heavy. Words cannot fully express how deeply I appreciate you.

Introduction
The Weight No One Sees

Everyone has an opinion about how a pastor should lead until they are the one carrying the cross of leadership.

People see the pulpit, the suit, the microphone, and the *amen* corner. What they do not see are the midnight prayers, the private tears, the disappointments, the betrayals, the sacrifices, and the crushing responsibility of shepherding souls.

This book is not written to discourage anyone from ministry. It is written to tell the truth.

Until you're the pastor, you're not.

You are not the one who feels the burn when the sheep scatter.

You are not the one who is both celebrated and criticized in the same breath.

You are not the one called to stand before God on behalf of souls.

Biblical leaders understood this weight. Moses bore the complaints of Israel. Paul carried the care of all the churches. Jesus Himself wept over Jerusalem because they "knew not the time of their visitation." Pastoring has never been glamorous. It is glory wrapped in suffering, an honor that carries a heavy cost.

What happens in ministry cannot always be seen from the pew. There are questions pastors carry that rarely get asked out loud. There are burdens they shoulder quietly, trusting God to strengthen them where applause cannot.

My prayer is simple.

That congregations gain understanding.

That aspiring leaders gain preparation.

That pastors, those already walking this road, can finally exhale and say, *"Someone understands."*

Chapter One
The Call You Didn't Choose

When God calls a pastor, He rarely asks for a résumé. He does not post a job description on a church bulletin board and wait for eager applicants to line up. He does not ask, "Who wants to suffer rejection, misunderstanding, and long nights of intercession?" Instead, He chooses. And when He chooses, He chooses according to His eternal plan, not our personal preferences.

I learned a long time ago that God does not consider our emotions or feelings when making decisions for our lives. It took many years for this truth to become a personal reality for me. This process is what makes the pastoral call both holy and heavy. It is a divine assignment that interrupts ordinary life. It is a summons that often collides with what we had planned for ourselves.

Many who now stand in pulpits once had very different dreams. Some were heading toward careers, businesses, or quiet lives in the background. But when God speaks, His voice cuts through the noise of human ambition and reroutes destiny.

Think of Moses. He did not volunteer to lead Israel. He had already fled Egypt, built a life in Midian, and likely assumed his story was finished. Yet at the burning bush, God disrupted his quiet exile with a call he never requested. Moses argued. He offered excuses. He begged God to choose someone else. Still, the call was nonnegotiable. The assignment had already been written in heaven.

Jeremiah felt the same weight. "Ah, Lord GOD! Behold, I cannot speak: for I am a child" (Jeremiah 1:6). His youth, his inadequacy, and his fear did not exempt him. God told him plainly, "Before I formed thee in the belly I knew thee, and before thou camest forth out of the womb I sanctified thee, and I ordained thee a prophet unto the nations" (Jeremiah 1:5). The call was sealed before his first breath.

That is the mystery. The pastoral call is not something you sign up for like a volunteer committee. It is something that overtakes you. Until you are the pastor, you may assume that leaders chase pulpits and titles. But when you are the pastor, you realize the opposite is true. The call chases you.

And with that call comes cost.

Abraham had to leave his father's house.

Elisha had to burn his plow and kiss his family goodbye.

Peter had to leave his nets and follow a Rabbi he barely understood.

The call of God always interrupts comfort.

This raises the first hard question. What happens when your yes to God dismantles your personal dreams? What if the life you imagined, the career, the quiet, the security, is swept away by the burden of souls? Until you are the pastor, you may not grasp how painful that surrender can be.

I gave God my yes in 2006. That was the moment my life changed forever. It was during that season that religious beliefs collided with Kingdom principles, and I began to truly see and understand the Word of God. I watched as it changed my thinking and my actions.

If it were up to me, I would have been a traveling reggae drummer. I was labeled as one of the best on my island home and enjoyed the popularity that came with playing and touring with multiple bands. I remember sitting back one day and asking myself, *How do I go to the next level?*

I wanted to be on the stage. I wanted to travel to different cities, towns, and countries. I wanted to be surrounded by large monitors, hearing every tap echo back through the speakers, mixed perfectly with the keys and singers. I wanted to feel the bass guitar pounding against my chest with every note.

I thought of my favorite artist, Beres Hammond, and began to brainstorm how I could audition for his famous band, Harmony House. The more I thought about the possibilities, the more the desire grew. Anticipation and eagerness built until it reached a full crescendo.

I was good at what I did. I was gifted, and I knew God had given me that gift. I was convinced that I was designed to hold a pair of drumsticks in my hands, make a great living, and travel the world doing what I loved.

Ultimately, God had other plans.

My yes to God became His no to my dreams, and that no led me straight into my calling.

Can you remain faithful to a call you never chose?

Moses did not volunteer. Jeremiah did not sign up. Even Jesus, in His humanity, wrestled with the cup in Gethsemane. The test of true pastoral leadership is not willingness at the beginning, but obedience all the way through.

This is why Paul could say, "Woe is unto me, if I preach not the gospel!" (1 Corinthians 9:16). The call is not an option to be considered. It is an assignment to be carried. Once you are chosen, running is futile. Jonah discovered that the hard way. He boarded a ship in rebellion, but God stirred a storm until Jonah's no became a surrendered yes.

The pastor's call is not glamorous. It is not a hobby. It is not the next rung on a ladder of ambition. It is an unshakable appointment from heaven.

And until you sit under that weight, until you feel the disruption, the cost, and the relentless pursuit of God's hand on your life, you may not understand why pastors carry both glory and grief in their eyes.

The truth is simple.

You do not choose this life.

This life chooses you.

Chapter Two
The Affliction That Shapes You

eadership looks crowded from the outside. People see the pastor surrounded by a congregation, embraced after service, prayed for, and celebrated during anniversaries. But when the public layer is peeled back, there is often a soul wrestling in solitude. No matter how many voices cheer in the sanctuary, there are burdens of leadership that can only be carried alone.

Moses understood this well. Imagine standing before a multitude who had just walked through the Red Sea, yet murmured against you at every inconvenience. He could not turn to the congregation for comfort because they were the source of his frustration. His only outlet was to fall before God and cry out, "Wherefore hast thou afflicted thy servant... that thou layest the burden of all this people upon me?" (Numbers 11:11). That is the cry of a lonely leader.

Elijah felt it too. After calling down fire from heaven and defeating the prophets of Baal, one would expect affirmation to follow. Instead, he fled into the wilderness and prayed to die. "I, even I only, am left," he lamented (1 Kings 19:10). In his mind, no one understood, no one carried the weight, no one stood with him. Loneliness spoke louder than victory.

Even Jesus endured this isolation. He walked with twelve disciples, yet in Gethsemane, when He asked them to pray with Him, they slept. In His greatest hour of need, the ones closest to Him could not share the weight. The Son of God, Emmanuel, God with us, knew the crushing solitude of leadership.

This is one of the great misunderstandings of pastoring. People often confuse proximity with intimacy. A pastor can be surrounded by people and still feel deeply alone. Congregants may love the gift but miss the heart. They desire the Word, the prayer, the blessing, yet never notice the tears behind the sermon, the weariness behind the smile, or the loneliness behind the strong handshake.

Until you're the pastor, you may not recognize the paradox. You are visible to all, yet deeply unknown by most. You pour yourself out for others but cannot always share your own struggles. You stand before the congregation each week, but who stands before God on your behalf?

How do you lead people who love your gift but misunderstand your heart?

People are drawn to the gift of a pastor. They admire the preaching, the teaching, the wisdom, and the ability to inspire. They gather to hear the gift, line up to receive from the gift, and applaud the gift. But the heart is different. The heart aches when members drift away. The heart prays over wayward souls at midnight. The heart longs to be known, not just needed. And here lies the ache. Some will celebrate the oil on your life while never perceiving the humanity beneath it.

Moses lived this tension. Israel loved his gift when seas parted and water flowed from rocks, but they misunderstood his heart when they accused him of leading them into the wilderness to die. David experienced it too. The people sang of his victories, but when pressure mounted, they spoke of stoning him (1 Samuel 30:6).

So how does a pastor lead within this tension? By remembering that leadership is not about being understood. It is about being faithful. God never promised that His shepherds would be fully known by their sheep. Jesus Himself was misunderstood by His own disciples, even though His love for them was unquestionable. The pastor leads for God, not applause. And when the heart is misunderstood, that ache must be poured back into prayer, echoing David's cry, "Search me, O God, and know my heart" (Psalm 139:23). The One who called you is the only One who fully knows you.

Another question presses in. What do you do when you cannot confide in the congregation, and you dare not burden your family?

This is where the pastoral road narrows. The people you pour into cannot always carry your private battles. Some truths, if spoken, would shake their faith or be mishandled. And while your family loves you, they should not bear the crushing weight of ministry's spiritual warfare. To overburden them risks bitterness in a spouse or children toward the very church you are called to serve.

So what does the pastor do? First, the pastor learns to confide in God with raw honesty. Like Hannah, pouring out her soul before the Lord, the pastor brings groanings that no human ear can interpret. Prayer stops being polite and becomes survival.

Second, God often provides safe confidants outside the immediate circle. This may be a seasoned mentor, a trusted spiritual father or mother, or another pastor who understands the terrain. Paul had Barnabas. Moses had Jethro. Even Jesus had an inner circle who walked further with Him in moments of pressure. Third, the pastor develops rhythms of unburdening through rest. Silence can be sacred. Jesus withdrew to solitary places not because He lacked love for people, but because He needed renewal in the Father's presence. Sabbath, retreat, and rest are not luxuries. They are lifelines.

At the core of pastoral life is this question. Who shepherds the shepherd? The answer is layered. God does. Trusted mentors do. Wise peers do. And often, the pastor learns to dwell in holy solitude where God Himself becomes confessor, comforter, and counselor.

Another question emerges. What does it cost your soul to always be the encourager when you need encouragement yourself?

Every pastor knows this tension. You stand in the pulpit declaring, "Weeping may endure for a night, but joy comes in the morning," while midnight still lingers in your own soul. You hug the grieving, speak life to the discouraged, and pray healing for the sick, then go home carrying unanswered prayers and silent tears. Pastors are human, yet rarely permitted to appear weak. The encourager cannot look discouraged. The shepherd cannot appear shaken. People need strength, so you give it, even when it drains your last reserve.

I often say, "God, You have a sense of humor." There are moments when I am dealing with private battles involving family, health, finances, or personal pain, and God sends someone wrestling with the very thing I am enduring. In those moments, I must set myself aside and offer prayer, wisdom, and comfort. That is the weight of the call.

Paul captured this paradox when he wrote, "We are troubled on every side, yet not distressed; we are perplexed, but not in despair; persecuted, but not forsaken" (2 Corinthians 4:8–9). He acknowledged the struggle while still strengthening others. That is the pastor's dilemma, carrying battle and blessing in the same breath.

There is a hidden cost. If the pastor never receives encouragement, the well eventually runs dry. The encourager can begin to feel invisible, valued only for what they give, not for who they are. That unseen drain can lead to fatigue, bitterness, and burnout. Elijah beneath the juniper tree was not only tired from ministry. He was tired from encouraging people who poured little back into him.

So what sustains a pastor? The Word becomes both mirror and medicine. Often, the sermons preached to others are first preached by God to the pastor's own weary heart. Encouragement is also found in God's presence. As David declared, "I encouraged myself in the Lord" (1 Samuel 30:6). And encouragement appears in glimpses of fruit. The prodigal returns. A marriage is restored. A soul grows under the Word. These moments remind the pastor that their labor is not in vain.

Still, the cost remains. To always be the encourager is to live in a constant outpouring. Until you're the pastor, you may not understand how exhausting it is to lift others while your own arms tremble. That is why pastors treasure small gestures of care. A sincere thank you. An unexpected prayer. A moment of encouragement. In those rare moments, the encourager is reminded that they, too, are loved.

Pastoring can feel like living on an island while the world watches from the shore. People see sermons and leadership, but the private reality is frequent solitude. Yet this loneliness is often God's proving ground. Moses met God alone on the mountain. Elijah heard the still, small voice only after retreating to a cave. Jesus emerged from forty days in the wilderness with clarity and power. Solitude refines leaders in ways community cannot.

The loneliness of leadership is painful, but it is purposeful. In those quiet hours, pastors encounter God in depths the crowd will never know. Faith is forged there. Vision is clarified there. Dependence on God becomes absolute.

Until you are the pastor, you may not understand why leaders withdraw, why they walk heavily after powerful services, or why their eyes reveal a sorrow they never voice. But when you are the pastor, you learn this truth.

Loneliness is not weakness.

It is part of the weight of the call.

And in that solitude, the pastor discovers the one Companion who never slumbers, never betrays, and never misunderstands. The loneliness of leadership is real, but so is the promise of the Lord who said, "Lo, I am with you always, even unto the end of the world" (Matthew 28:20).

Chapter Three
The Burden of Souls

A pastor does not simply carry a title. A pastor carries souls. That is the invisible burden, one that cannot be measured in spreadsheets, bulletins, or church growth statistics. Hebrews 13:17 states it plainly. Pastors "watch for your souls, as they that must give account." That verse alone should cause any casual observer to pause. To be accountable to God for eternal souls is no small weight.

Paul understood this burden deeply. In 2 Corinthians 11:28, after listing shipwrecks, beatings, hunger, and betrayal, he adds, "And besides those things that are without, there is the daily pressure of my care for all the churches." For Paul, the physical suffering was severe, but the heavier load was internal. It was the constant care of souls. He felt the weight of seeing Christ formed in people, of worrying for the weak, of praying for those drifting, and of protecting those vulnerable to spiritual attack. That pressure pressed harder than lashes or prisons ever could.

Every true pastor recognizes this feeling. It is the constant awareness that eternity hangs in the balance for those under your watch. When the congregation dismisses and goes home, they may carry personal concerns such as bills, jobs, and family matters. The pastor carries not only their own household and personal struggles, but the collective burden of souls. The one who strays. The one whose faith is fragile. The one whose heart is bitter. The one who sits in the pew smiling, yet goes home battling thoughts of despair.

This is why pastoring is unlike any other form of leadership. A CEO carries employees. A coach carries players. A pastor carries souls. And the soul is the most precious thing in the universe. Heaven rejoices over one that repents. Christ gave His life to redeem it. That is the true measure of the weight.

In real life, this burden looks very different from what people imagine. It looks like sleepless nights when a member has gone missing and your spirit will not rest until you reach them. It looks like wrestling in prayer until exhaustion sets in because you sense a spiritual assignment against someone under your covering. It looks like quietly grieving when someone backslides, not because they disappointed you, but because you understand the cost to their soul.

Until you're the pastor, these hidden battles often go unseen. You may only see the Sunday sermon. But behind every message is a heart that has carried people in prayer all week. Behind every altar call is a pastor pleading, "Lord, do not let them leave unchanged." Behind every word of counsel is the sober awareness that this soul is eternal and must be handled with care.

This raises questions outsiders rarely ask.

How does it feel to carry responsibility for eternal souls while still working out your own salvation with fear and trembling?

This is the paradox of pastoring. You are shepherd and sheep at the same time. You stand before God's people to guide them, yet you kneel before God as one desperate for His grace yourself. Paul acknowledged this tension when he wrote that he disciplined his own body, lest after preaching to others, he himself should be disqualified (1 Corinthians 9:27).

It is a sobering reality. Pastors preach against sin they themselves must resist. They urge others to remain faithful while wrestling with weariness. They call people to prayer while guarding their own devotional lives with discipline. The pastor is not exempt from spiritual warfare. They are simply called to lead through it.

This reality produces deep humility. No matter how many people a pastor shepherds, they remain first a soul accountable to God. Every sermon is preached with the awareness that the Word cuts the preacher first. Every altar call echoes back into the pastor's own heart. Until you're the pastor, you may not understand the weight of calling others higher while still climbing yourself.

Another question follows closely behind.

Do people realize that their pastor loses sleep not over numbers or programs, but over salvation?

Many assume pastors lie awake worrying about attendance charts, budgets, or building projects. But the truth is far more personal. A pastor's sleeplessness is tied to faces and names, not statistics. It comes from the teenager quietly slipping away, the marriage on the brink, the saint growing cold in worship.

Numbers can be managed. Souls cannot. Numbers are replaceable. Souls are eternal. That is why pastors awaken in the early hours of the morning with a member's name heavy on their spirit. That is why they pace floors praying in groans no one else hears. That is why they can look weary even during seasons of numerical growth, because numbers can rise while souls still slip through unseen cracks.

Paul described this burden as travail, saying he labored again until Christ was formed in believers (Galatians 4:19). His language mirrors childbirth. Pastors carry that same labor. Their rest is not disrupted by logistics, but by love. Until you're the pastor, you may not realize that true success is not measured in filled pews, but in secured souls.

And what does it do to a pastor's heart when one sheep wanders while the ninety-nine assume it is no big deal?

Jesus addressed this directly in Luke 15. He described leaving the ninety-nine to pursue the one lost sheep. This was not merely a parable. It revealed the heart of a shepherd. The crowd may overlook the one, but the pastor cannot. The burden of souls demands pursuit, intercession, and sacrifice.

Here lies another hidden cost. No matter how faithfully a pastor prays, preaches, or counsels, each soul must ultimately choose for itself. A pastor can point toward life, but people may still choose otherwise. That tension is heartbreaking. To give everything you have, only to watch some turn away. Even Jesus experienced this pain. John 6 records that after one of His strongest teachings, many disciples walked away and followed Him no more.

What sustains a pastor beneath this immense weight is the knowledge that souls ultimately belong to God. The pastor is a steward, not an owner. The Good Shepherd alone carries final responsibility. This truth does not remove the weight, but it rightly frames it. A pastor must still answer for faithfulness, for preaching the Word, for warning, comforting, supporting, and loving God's people with patience.

Until you're the pastor, you may not realize that the heaviest thing a pastor carries is not the church mortgage, the calendar, or the staff. The heaviest thing is eternal. It is invisible. It is the soul of the one sitting in front of them.

And it is this weight that drives pastors to their knees more than anything else, because they know what is truly at stake.

Chapter Four
When the Sheep Bite

If pastoring were only about preaching the Word, many would find it easy. But shepherding is never done in a vacuum. It happens in the presence of people, with their opinions, assumptions, and voices. While a pastor may carry the love of God in his heart, he must also carry the reality that not everyone will understand him. Some will misread his motives. Some will question his decisions. Some will openly criticize the very sacrifices he makes in secret.

Moses lived under constant criticism. He led Israel out of slavery by the power of God's hand, yet they grumbled against him again and again. At Marah when the water was bitter. In the wilderness when food was scarce. At Kadesh when the journey grew long. At every turn, his leadership was met with suspicion. In Numbers 16, Korah led a rebellion, accusing Moses of exalting himself over the people. Imagine the pain of being accused of pride when you never wanted the role to begin with.

Jesus Himself was misunderstood more than anyone. The crowds loved Him for His miracles, yet questioned His authority when His words cut too deeply. In Nazareth, His own hometown rejected Him, saying, "Is not this the carpenter's son?" (Matthew 13:55). They could not see past His humanity to perceive His divinity. Even His disciples often missed His heart, debating greatness while He prepared for the cross.

This is the sting pastors know all too well. Being loved for the gift but judged for humanity. Being celebrated one week and criticized the next. Being praised for a decision until it costs something, then accused of failure.

Until you're the pastor, you may not realize how deep these wounds go. It is not the criticism of strangers that cuts the most. It is the criticism of those you have prayed for, counseled, wept over, and served with your whole heart.

This leads to a hard question.

Can you survive when the very people you serve turn against you?

It is a test every pastor faces. The people you feed can be the first to bite. The ones you fight for can become the ones who fight you. The issue is not whether this will happen, but how you will endure when it does. Moses fell on his face before God when rebellion rose up. David strengthened himself in the Lord when his own men talked of stoning him (1 Samuel 30:6). Jesus, in the face of betrayal and denial, pressed forward to Calvary. Survival is not found in defending yourself, but in anchoring yourself in God's presence. If you live by applause, you will die by criticism.

Another question follows closely behind.

What do you do when criticism is louder than gratitude?

This is one of the oldest melodies in ministry. Gratitude whispers, but criticism shouts. You can pour out your life like Paul, "being poured out like a drink offering" (2 Timothy 4:6), and the congregation nods politely. But the first time you miss a detail, stumble in delivery, or make a decision that unsettles people, the volume of criticism rises sharply.

Here is the irony. You may receive nine expressions of thanks in a week, but it is the one critical sentence that replays in your mind at two in the morning. Gratitude fades into the background, while criticism becomes the soundtrack.

Jesus modeled this reality. Of the ten lepers healed, only one returned with gratitude (Luke 17:11–19). That means the Son of God experienced a ninety percent ingratitude rate. If Christ Himself encountered more silence than thanks, His servants should not expect an easier road.

So what does a pastor do? You resist letting people's volume determine your value. If your worth depends on applause, you will collapse when the room grows quiet. If you live for approval, rejection will undo you. Pastors must learn to tune their ear to the right frequency. The shepherd listens not only to the sheep, but to the voice of the Chief Shepherd. God's "Well done, good and faithful servant" (Matthew 25:23) must outweigh the crowd's fickle chorus.

Gratitude is a gift, but it cannot be your fuel. It is welcome when it comes, but unreliable. Obedience must be the source of strength. Jesus said, "My food is to do the will of Him who sent Me and to finish His work" (John 4:34). That nourishment sustains when affirmation runs dry.

There is also this perspective. Criticism often confirms that you are doing something that matters. No one throws stones at a barren tree. They throw them at one bearing fruit. The noise may signal that people are being stretched in uncomfortable ways.

So when criticism grows louder than gratitude, do not waste energy amplifying the whispers. Tune your heart to the eternal voice where heaven's applause never fades. Gratitude may come in moments, but glory belongs to God. You were not called to be popular. You were called to be faithful.

This leads to another difficult question.

How does a leader develop thick skin without a hard heart?

This may be the hardest lesson of all. To survive criticism, resilience is necessary. But to remain Christlike, that resilience cannot harden into bitterness. Thick skin protects you from offense. A hard heart separates you from compassion. Pastoring requires strength and tenderness to exist together. You are called to love the people, teach the people, and lead the people, while also being firm enough to stand when they resist.

The balance is delicate. You learn to hear criticism without allowing it to poison you. You absorb misunderstanding without letting it embitter you. Jesus modeled this balance on the cross when He prayed, "Father, forgive them; for they know not what they do" (Luke 23:34). His body bore lashes. His soul bore betrayal. Yet His heart remained soft enough to forgive.

For the pastor, this means guarding the heart in prayer. Refusing to let bitterness settle. Remembering that sheep are sheep. Often they bite not out of malice, but immaturity. And still, you love. Because a shepherd without love is no shepherd at all.

Criticism and misunderstanding are unavoidable companions in ministry, but they are also refining fires. They strip away ego, drive leaders into deeper dependence on God, and test whether love is conditional or Christlike. Until you're the pastor, leadership may seem like admiration. But when you are the pastor, you discover it is about faithfulness, even when you are misunderstood.

The art, then, is this. Allow God to toughen your exterior while continually inviting Him to tenderize your interior. That way, you can keep hugging the sheep, even when their wool hides sharp teeth.

Chapter Five
The Sacrifice Nobody Applauds

People often celebrate the pulpit but rarely see the price behind it. They admire the sermon without realizing what it cost the pastor to stand there. Ministry is not free. It costs time, tears, energy, relationships, and sometimes health. The pulpit may look like a platform of honor, but it is built on sacrifice. The world loves the sound of ministry without acknowledging the strain that produces it.

The apostle Paul said it plainly: "I will very gladly spend and be spent for you; though the more abundantly I love you, the less I be loved" (2 Corinthians 12:15). That is the paradox of pastoring. You pour yourself out completely for people who may never see the cost, may never say thank you, and may never love you back. Until you're the pastor, you may not realize how many sacrifices go unnoticed.

The Sacrifice of Time

Pastoring is not a nine-to-five job. It is a twenty-four-hour calling. Births, deaths, crises, and emergencies do not consult a calendar.

Pastors miss dinners, anniversaries, children's games, and often their own rest. The sheep may see the one hour on Sunday, but they rarely see the other six days when the pastor lays down his life in a hundred unseen ways through late-night prayers, hospital visits, and emergency counseling.

Moses judged the people from morning until evening (Exodus 18:13), to the point that Jethro warned him he would wear himself out. David echoed the same heart when he declared, "I will not give sleep to mine eyes… until I find out a place for the Lord" (Psalm 132:4–5). This is the heartbeat of a shepherd, one who loses sleep for the sake of the sheep.

The Sacrifice of Family

This may be the hardest sacrifice of all. Pastors' families often live in a glass house. Their children grow up under scrutiny. Their spouses carry heavy burdens without the same voice or recognition. Many family moments are interrupted or shortened because the needs of the congregation intervene.

Consider Samuel. His sons did not walk in his ways, yet the people judged Samuel for their failures (1 Samuel 8:1–5). David's family bore the weight of his calling as well. Michal despised him for his worship. Absalom rebelled against him. Solomon inherited both his crown and his conflicts. Every pastor silently asks, *What will this calling cost my family?* And yet they serve anyway, entrusting those they love most into the hands of the God who called them.

The Sacrifice of Self

Paul said, "I die daily" (1 Corinthians 15:31). Pastoring is not about self-fulfillment. It is about self-denial. Dreams are laid down. Comforts are surrendered. Personal desires are delayed or denied for the sake of the Kingdom.

Elijah knew the loneliness of sacrifice when he sat under the juniper tree, weary from carrying the burden alone. Jeremiah knew it when he was thrown into a pit for speaking truth. Jesus knew it in Gethsemane when His soul was "exceeding sorrowful, even unto death" (Matthew 26:38). To lead God's people is to lay yourself on the altar daily, and the hardest part is that most will never see it, never know it, and never applaud it.

The Probing Questions of Sacrifice

How does it feel to carry responsibility for eternal souls while still working out your own salvation with fear and trembling?

Paul exhorted believers to "work out your own salvation with fear and trembling" (Philippians 2:12). That task alone is weighty. Now imagine doing it while also shepherding hundreds of others, each with their own struggles, temptations, and eternal destinies. It is like trying to build an ark while floodwaters are already rising. Noah was not only responsible for himself. He had to keep his family and every creature alive.

This is the tension pastors live with daily. They are still learning how to stay afloat while throwing life preservers to everyone else. There is no luxury of private struggle. People expect the pastor to have spiritually arrived, even while he presses toward the mark like Paul (Philippians 3:14). The true weight is not perfection, but accountability. Hebrews 13:17 reminds us that pastors watch over souls as those who must give an account. It is difficult to tremble for yourself when you are already trembling for others.

Do people realize that their pastor loses sleep not over numbers or programs, but over salvation?

Ask a faithful shepherd what keeps them awake at night. It is not whether the choir sang well or whether the logo looks modern on social media. It is whether Brother James is slipping back into addiction. It is whether Sister Ruth will survive grief without losing her faith. It is whether the teenager in the back row is hearing truth before other voices shape their beliefs.

Paul described this burden as labor, saying, "I labor in birth again until Christ is formed in you" (Galatians 4:19). That language speaks of pain, groaning, and restless nights. Moses carried the same agony when he pleaded, "If You will not forgive their sin, blot me out of Your book" (Exodus 32:32). He was not worried about numbers or resources. He was bargaining his life for theirs. Pastors may not always say it aloud, but their insomnia is often intercession.

What does it do to a pastor's heart when one sheep wanders and the ninety-nine assume it is no big deal?

Jesus told the story of the shepherd who left the ninety-nine to go after the one (Luke 15:4). Congregations applaud the parable, but pastors live the ache in real time. The heartbreak is not only that someone wandered. It is that the ninety-nine shrug and say, "People come and go." Not to a shepherd.

To a true pastor, every soul has a name, a story, and a testimony still being written. Losing one feels like losing a limb. David's cry over Absalom reveals this pain. When the battle ended and Absalom was dead, David did not celebrate victory. He wept, "O my son Absalom... If only I had died in your place!" (2 Samuel 18:33). That is the cry of a shepherd's heart.

The ninety-nine may be content with the crowd still intact, but the shepherd is pierced by the absence of the one. That wound lingers, because every empty seat echoes louder in the pastor's heart than full pews ever could.

Chapter Six
The Weight of Vision

Seeing What Others Cannot

Every pastor knows that vision is more than a dream or a good idea. Vision is a divine mandate. It is the physical manifestation of a spiritual revelation. It is fire shut up in your bones, a glimpse of God's heart for His people that He entrusts to you. While vision inspires, it also weighs heavily. Until you're the pastor, you may not realize that vision is both a gift and a burden. It lifts your spirit by showing you where God intends to take His people, yet it bends your back under the responsibility of leading them there.

Moses understood this weight. He stood on Mount Nebo and looked out over the Promised Land. He could see the vision clearly, but leading a stubborn, murmuring people through the wilderness nearly broke him. More than once, he cried out to God, "I am not able to bear all this people alone, because it is too heavy for me" (Numbers 11:14). The vision was glorious, but the mantle was crushing.

Nehemiah carried the same burden. He saw a rebuilt Jerusalem in his spirit long before a single stone was laid. That vision drove him to weep, fast, pray, and risk his life before kings. And Jesus Himself carried the greatest vision of all. He saw the joy set before Him, but to reach it, He endured the cross. Vision always carries a cross.

To the congregation, vision often looks like a plan, a program, or a slogan printed on a banner. To the pastor, it looks like sleepless nights, fervent prayer, and a holy dissatisfaction with mediocrity in God's house. People cheer the fruit of vision but resist the process of bringing it to life. They love the harvest but avoid the plow. They want the Promised Land, yet shrink back at the sight of giants.

This is the unseen tension pastors live with. You carry the distance between what is and what must be. I understand the implications of being a visionary. I can see what God has planned, but once I finish looking, I return to reality and face the truth that I still have to build it.

Here lies another layer of leadership's solitude. Not everyone sees what you see. Vision separates you. It makes you different. Noah knew this when he built an ark while his neighbors mocked him. Joseph knew it when he shared dreams of greatness and was rewarded with a pit and a prison. Visionaries often feel foolish long before they feel validated. Yet obedience demands that you build anyway, dream anyway, and move forward anyway. Vision is not optional. It is obedience.

This leads to difficult questions pastors must live with.

What do you do when you see a future your people cannot yet imagine?

You lead anyway. That is the agony and glory of leadership. You live miles ahead of the flock. Moses carried a vision of milk and honey while Israel longed for Egypt's onions (Numbers 11:5). He saw giants falling while they only saw giants standing. Pastors often carry a future pulsing with revival while others worry about surface-level concerns. The task is not to repeat what people see, but to declare what God has spoken. Habakkuk 2:3 reminds us that vision has an appointed time. It may tarry, but it will come. Vision makes you both prophet and punching bag. If people could already imagine it, they would not need you to lead them into it.

And sometimes, just to keep your sanity, you have to smile and say, "Lord, if Moses dragged millions through the desert, I suppose I can handle a handful in a board meeting."

Another question follows.

How do you keep carrying vision when others resist, misunderstand, or even sabotage it?

You carry it because God did not give it to them. He gave it to you. Joseph's dreams attracted resistance long before they produced authority. Vision exposes small thinking, and that makes people uncomfortable. It hurts when those you love misread passion as arrogance or persistence as stubbornness. Nehemiah shows us the response. When mocked, threatened, and opposed, he simply declared, "I am doing a great work, and I cannot come down" (Nehemiah 6:3). That resolve must live in every pastor's spirit. Vision is not about being understood. It is about being faithful.

You build even when resistance rises, sometimes holding a sword in one hand and a trowel in the other.

Another weight presses in.

What do you do when you believe for something you may never live to see fulfilled?

You plant anyway. Vision is generational. Abraham believed for a land he would never fully own. Moses saw Canaan from a mountain, but Joshua led the people in. David dreamed of the temple, but Solomon built it. God has no issue letting you draw the blueprints while someone else cuts the ribbon. Your legacy is not diminished by starting what you cannot finish. It is confirmed by obedience.

Pastors often wrestle with this quietly. What if I labor my whole life and never see the revival I prayed for? Hebrews 11 answers that fear. Many died in faith, having seen the promises from afar. Visionaries do not die disappointed. They die invested. You build as if it will happen tomorrow and believe even if it takes generations. In the Kingdom, obedience is the true fulfillment.

Vision costs. It costs friendships, because not everyone wants to walk where you are walking. It costs comfort, because sacrifice is required to move forward. It costs tears, because vision is often carried alone. Yet vision also rewards. It sharpens faith, inspires others, and secures legacy. Abraham's faith laid the foundation for nations.

The weight of vision is proof that God trusts you with something eternal. He does not reveal vision casually. He entrusts it carefully. As Habakkuk declared, "Write the vision, and make it plain"

(Habakkuk 2:2). What God reveals, He sustains. What God ordains, He provides for. The pastor's role is not to invent vision, but to steward it.

The weight is real, but so is the grace. And when vision finally blossoms, when lives are changed and souls are saved, you realize it was worth every tear, every lonely night, and every misunderstood moment.

Vision is heavy, but it is holy. And until you're the pastor, you may never understand the crushing beauty of carrying God's dream in your chest.

Chapter Seven
The Burden of Expectations

If vision is heavy, expectations can feel suffocating. A pastor is called to shepherd souls, yet people often expect more than God ever required. They want you to be preacher, counselor, administrator, fundraiser, mediator, therapist, event planner, marriage guru, financial coach, and sometimes even a miracle worker, all at once. Until you're the pastor, you may not realize how impossible those expectations truly are.

The congregation may love their pastor, but they often forget that he or she is flesh and blood. Pastors get tired. Pastors get discouraged. Pastors have families, bills, weaknesses, and limits. Yet people frequently prefer their pastor to appear superhuman. They want strength without struggle, wisdom without wrestling, and compassion without boundaries. Paul experienced this tension when the Corinthians elevated him one moment and questioned his authority the next. Jesus faced it as well. Crowds adored His miracles, yet many abandoned Him at the cross. This is the burden of expectations: to be celebrated for what you provide, but rarely permitted to be fully human.

There is another truth not often spoken. Many pastors live under a constant fear of disappointing people. A missed call, an overlooked hospital visit, or a decision that does not please everyone can quickly turn into criticism, gossip, or even division. All of this pressure exists while the pastor is still trying to discern and obey what God actually said. Pastors lose sleep not over titles or recognition, but over whether they failed someone. They carry the quiet weight of comparison, measured against the former pastor, the popular online preacher, or an ideal shepherd that exists only in imagination.

This leads to questions every pastor must wrestle with.

How do you balance God's call with people's demands?

The honest answer is that you do not, at least not perfectly. Pastoral life exists in constant tension between what God has spoken and what people want. Moses lived this reality daily. God called him to lead Israel toward Canaan, yet the people demanded water, food, comfort, and reassurance, often delivered rudely and without gratitude (Numbers 20:2–5). The pressure nearly broke him. At one point he cried out, "Did I conceive all these people? Did I give them birth? Why do you tell me to carry them in my arms?" (Numbers 11:12). That is not the voice of weakness. It is the voice of a leader crushed beneath endless expectations.

The balance is found by remembering who called you. If you spend your life trying to meet every demand, you will burn out faster than Elijah beneath the broom tree (1 Kings 19:4). But when you anchor yourself in God's call, something freeing happens. You realize you are not responsible to fulfill every demand. You are responsible to obey God's voice. People will always have opinions about how you should spend your time, but the moment you try to please everyone, you end up pleasing no one, especially not God.

Another question follows closely.

What do you do when expectations exceed your capacity?

The answer is simple to say and difficult to live. You admit your limits. You are not God. You are not omnipresent, omniscient, or omnipotent. You are human, with a body that needs rest and a spirit that needs renewal. Jesus Himself modeled this truth. Crowds pursued Him relentlessly, yet He withdrew regularly to solitary places to pray (Luke 5:16). The Son of God left some needs unmet because He understood His human capacity. If Jesus was not afraid to disappoint expectations, pastors should not feel guilty for doing the same.

The apostles reinforced this wisdom in Acts 6. When the early church expected them to manage both the ministry of the Word and food distribution, they responded clearly. It would not be right to neglect the Word of God to wait on tables (Acts 6:2). They did not deny the need. They delegated it. Capacity is not merely about what you can do. It is about what you are called to do. Without boundaries, a pastor pours out until nothing remains, and an empty vessel cannot shepherd anyone.

This raises another tension.

When is it obedience to serve people, and when is it obedience to disappoint them for the sake of God's will?

Sometimes obedience means sacrificial service. Jesus washed feet. Paul became a servant to all so that he might win more (John 13:5; 1 Corinthians 9:19). Serving people is obedience when it reflects the heart of Christ. But there are moments when obedience requires holy disappointment. When Peter tried to steer Jesus away from the cross, Jesus rebuked him sharply, because pleasing Peter would have derailed God's plan (Matthew 16:23).

Pastoral wisdom discerns the difference. Serving people is obedience when it leads them closer to God. Disappointing people is obedience when their expectations would pull you away from Him. Samuel learned this when Israel demanded a king. Though Samuel grieved, God reminded him, "They have not rejected you, but they have rejected Me" (1 Samuel 8:7). Sometimes obedience means allowing disappointment, not because you failed, but because the demand itself fell outside God's design.

Unrealistic expectations take a toll. They breed guilt, anxiety, resentment, and exhaustion. They isolate leaders and push them toward burnout. Elijah collapsed beneath the juniper tree not only because Jezebel threatened him, but because the weight of expectation drained him. Moses nearly lost his calling when frustration drove him to strike the rock. Expectations left unchecked can derail even the strongest shepherd.

But there is grace here. God never called pastors to be everything. He called them to be faithful. Faithful to His Word. Faithful to His voice. Faithful to the souls entrusted to their care. Paul wrote, "It is required in stewards that one be found faithful" (1 Corinthians 4:2). Not flawless. Not omnipresent. Faithful.

Freedom comes when a pastor releases the burden of impossible standards and carries only what God assigns. That freedom is obedience. That obedience is survival.

The burden of expectations will always hover, but the wise pastor learns to set boundaries, lean on the team God provides, and remember this truth. You cannot please all people, but you can please the One who called you.

Until you're the pastor, you may not understand how exhausting it is to be everything others want. But you will understand how freeing it is to be exactly what God asked you to be.

Chapter Eight
The Battle with Loneliness

A crowded sanctuary does not cure a lonely soul. Many assume that because a pastor is constantly surrounded by people, he or she could not possibly feel alone. Yet some of the loneliest hours a person will ever experience are lived within the pastorate. Until you're the pastor, you may not understand how a leader can stand in the middle of a crowd, shaking hands and smiling, while feeling profoundly isolated inside.

Leadership itself is isolating. When you carry the mantle of shepherding God's people, there are burdens you cannot share and decisions only you can make. There are nights when you wrestle with God while everyone else sleeps peacefully. Moses expressed this isolation when he cried out, "I am not able to bear all this people alone, because it is too heavy for me" (Numbers 11:14). Though surrounded by thousands, he felt utterly alone.

Jesus Himself experienced this reality. Though crowds followed Him, He often withdrew to solitary places to pray. And in His darkest hour, the garden of Gethsemane, His closest disciples could not stay awake with Him. He faced betrayal, denial, and abandonment, not from strangers, but from friends. Loneliness is not foreign to leadership; it is woven into its fabric.

Pastors battle loneliness for very real reasons. They cannot always confide in the congregation, because sharing too much may shake confidence. They dare not overburden their families, who already live beneath the shadow of the calling. And few truly understand the weight a pastor carries. The pastor listens to everyone's struggles, yet rarely has space to voice their own. This creates a painful paradox. The pastor is surrounded, yet secluded. Accessible, yet unseen.

This leads to the question many pastors quietly carry.

Who shepherds the shepherd?

It is the question beneath all the others. People assume the pastor is a well that never runs dry. But even a well needs a source, and when that source is neglected, the well empties. David understood this. Though he was a king, a warrior, and a leader of men, he introduced himself in Psalm 23 simply as a sheep. "The Lord is my Shepherd." Before David led anyone else, he acknowledged that he himself was being led.

Pastors often forget this. In feeding others, they starve themselves. Yet Psalm 23 reminds us that even shepherds need green pastures and still waters. Even shepherds need restoration of the soul. Even shepherds need comfort. The truth is simple. If you believe you can shepherd others without being shepherded yourself, you are not strong. You are exhausted and approaching collapse.

Another question surfaces.

Where does the pastor go when the pastor's soul is weary?

Elijah went to the wilderness. He collapsed beneath a broom tree and prayed to die (1 Kings 19:4). That was not a public testimony moment. It was burnout laid bare. God did not rebuke him. He sent an angel, provided food, and commanded him to rest. Sometimes the most spiritual act a pastor can perform is to eat, sleep, and recover.

Jeremiah went to the depths of despair, crying out, "Cursed be the day I was born!" (Jeremiah 20:14). He preached faithfully and was mocked relentlessly. His refuge was not affirmation, but the fire of God's calling burning in his bones (Jeremiah 20:9). Jesus went to the garden. In Gethsemane, He admitted, "My soul is overwhelmed with sorrow to the point of death" (Matthew 26:38). He did not hide His anguish. He carried it straight to the Father in prayer. If the Son of God needed to wrestle His weary soul before God, pastors should never feel ashamed to do the same.

So where does the pastor go when weary? To the One who never grows weary. "The everlasting God, the Lord, fainteth not, neither is weary" (Isaiah 40:28).

Another paradox remains.

How do you keep ministering to others when your own heart longs for a listening ear?

This is the tension of pastoral life. You pour into others while your own cup feels empty. Paul captured this when he wrote, "Sorrowful, yet always rejoicing; poor, yet making many rich; having nothing, and yet possessing everything" (2 Corinthians

6:10). Ministry often requires giving out of both abundance and emptiness.

But it is dangerous to live in constant output without input. Jesus warned that out of the abundance of the heart the mouth speaks (Matthew 12:34). When the heart runs dry, what eventually comes out is frustration, bitterness, or silence. Pastors must learn to replenish before depletion becomes damage.

Strength is sustained in several ways. First, by drawing directly from God. Paul pleaded for his thorn to be removed, but God replied, "My grace is sufficient for you" (2 Corinthians 12:9). Sometimes grace is the only supply available, and it is enough. Second, by cultivating safe relationships. Paul had Timothy, Luke, and Barnabas. Jesus had Peter, James, and John. Every pastor needs at least one or two people who see the human behind the pulpit. And third, by remembering a crucial truth. The pastor is not the Savior. That role is already filled. The pastor does not carry the cross. He points people to the One who already did.

Loneliness becomes dangerous when ignored. Left unchecked, it breeds discouragement, self-doubt, and temptation. Elijah's despair beneath the broom tree was fueled by the belief that he was the only one left (1 Kings 19:10). Isolation makes lies feel true. A lonely pastor is vulnerable spiritually, emotionally, and morally. The enemy thrives where leaders feel unseen.

But God never abandons His servants. To Elijah, He revealed that seven thousand faithful ones remained (1 Kings 19:18). The pastor is rarely as alone as he feels. Relief often comes through fellowship with God, trusted companions, and the abiding presence of the

Holy Spirit. When human encouragement is scarce, the Spirit becomes Comforter, Counselor, and constant Friend.

Loneliness is a shadow every pastor will face. Yet even in that shadow, God walks closely beside His servant. The crowd may not notice the isolation, but the Shepherd of shepherds never does.

Until you're the pastor, you may not understand how deeply loneliness haunts the role. But you will also discover how powerfully God uses that loneliness to draw His servant nearer to Himself.

Chapter Nine
The Poverty of Spirit (and Sometimes Wallet)

If there is one unspoken truth about ministry, it is this: shepherding God's people often costs more than it pays. Pastors carry not only the poverty of spirit, that blessed emptiness that keeps them dependent on God, but at times the poverty of provision as well. Ministry is not a profession padded with perks. It is a calling sustained by faith.

Jesus said, "Blessed are the poor in spirit, for theirs is the kingdom of heaven" (Matthew 5:3). Poverty of spirit means living in constant dependence, never presuming strength apart from God. Yet many pastors know another kind of poverty too, the financial strain of serving where offerings are slim, needs are great, and bills do not pause for prayer. This reality is rarely preached, but it is deeply lived.

The apostle Paul understood this tension well. Though called to plant churches and preach the gospel, he also stitched tents to support himself (Acts 18:3). He was not ashamed of it. His ministry was not powered by gold, but by grace. Paul could write honestly, "I have learned to be content whatever the circumstances. I know what it is to be in need, and I know what it is to have plenty" (Philippians 4:11–12). That testimony still echoes in the lives of many pastors who labor faithfully while their bank accounts tell a different story.

The prophets of old lived in this same tension. Elijah survived a famine not through royal provision, but through the obedience of a poor widow at Zarephath (1 Kings 17:9–16). Elisha was sustained by a Shunammite woman who built him a small room on her roof (2 Kings 4:8–10). God's servants were often supported not by abundance, but by sacrifice. Not by palaces, but by widows' bread. It is humbling to realize that God sometimes funds His mission not with surplus, but with trust.

This places pastors on a narrow tightrope between faith and provision. Faith declares, "God will supply all your needs" (Philippians 4:19), while the electric company sends a notice marked "Payment Due." Pastors do not serve for money, yet money remains part of the human reality. Their families feel the pressure. Their children grow up hearing sermons about God's abundance while watching their parents stretch every dollar. In those moments, poverty of spirit is no longer a theological concept. It becomes survival.

Modern ministry offers quiet pictures of this sacrifice. A pastor drives a second-hand car with hundreds of thousands of miles on it, not for leisure, but for hospital visits, counseling sessions, and late-night emergencies. Some mock the vehicle, unaware it has become a chariot of grace. A pastor's spouse clips coupons at the kitchen table while the sermon is prepared nearby. One labors to keep the fridge full. The other labors to keep the Word ready. Both callings are holy, and both are unseen.

There is also the pastor who quietly works a night shift, stocks shelves, drives deliveries, or picks up extra work so the congregation never knows how close the family is to the edge. By day, he preaches with fire. By night, he provides with weary hands. Few connect the two. Yet somehow, the bills get paid. Shoes appear for growing children. The lights stay on in both home and church. Manna still falls, never enough to hoard, but always enough to survive.

This reality raises hard questions.

How do you keep serving faithfully when ministry costs more than it gives?

This is the pastor's paradox. Pouring out when you already feel poured dry. Serving when the wallet is thin, energy stretched, and emotions running low. Paul captured this tension when he said, "I will most gladly spend and be spent for your souls" (2 Corinthians 12:15). Notice his word choice. Gladly. Not grudgingly. His faithfulness was rooted in obedience, not return.

There is honesty here too. It feels strange preaching abundance while staring at an overdue bill. Pastors are not immune to the dissonance between pulpit promises and kitchen-table realities. Yet they keep serving because they remember who called them. Eternal paychecks are not signed by people. Success is measured in faithfulness, not finances. And joy does not cost money. It costs surrender.

Another question presses even deeper.

How do you lead people into abundance while quietly battling lack?

This question stings because it feels like hypocrisy. How can you preach prosperity while scraping together gas money? But this is not hypocrisy. It is integrity under fire. Abundance is preached not because the wallet proves it, but because God's Word declares it. Moses led Israel toward a land flowing with milk and honey while he himself ate manna in the wilderness. Paul wrote of spiritual riches while chained in a Roman prison. Abundance has never been measured by bank statements.

Pastors do not point people to themselves. They point them to God. The shepherd does not say, "Look at my pasture." He says, "Follow me to His." Sometimes the pastor's lack becomes the strongest sermon, a living testimony that God's Word stands firm even when circumstances argue otherwise.

And finally, the question every pastor must answer quietly.

How do you rest in God's provision when your wallet tells another story?

This is where theology becomes survival. Philippians 4:19 promises supply, yet faith is tested when bills arrive. Rest comes by learning the difference between needs and wants. God promises provision, not luxury. Elijah received bread and water, not a feast. Rest comes by trusting God's timing. The widow's jar of oil never overflowed, but it never ran dry either (1 Kings 17:16). Rest also comes by remembering past provision. If God fed you yesterday, He will feed you tomorrow. Faith often grows by recalling old miracles more than chasing new ones.

God has a way of arriving just late enough to stretch faith, but never too late to let His servant starve.

The poverty of spirit, and yes sometimes wallet, is not punishment. It is a reminder that ministry was never designed to be sustained by human resources alone. God Himself is the pastor's portion. David declared, "The Lord is my shepherd; I shall not want" (Psalm 23:1). That does not promise luxury, but it does promise sufficiency.

So if you serve and feel the pinch, know this. You stand in the company of prophets, apostles, and Christ Himself, who had nowhere to lay His head. Poverty may press you, but it will not crush you. For even in want, you are rich. Rich in calling. Rich in purpose. Rich in a Kingdom that cannot be measured in dollars or cents.

Conclusion
The Silent Weight, the Steady Hand

There is a silence in leadership that words rarely capture. It is not the hush of an empty room, but the solitude of a soul carrying a weight few can see. And yet, within that silence, a deeper voice speaks, the voice of the Shepherd who called you.

Throughout this book, we have journeyed through valleys together. Valleys of affliction and misunderstanding. Valleys of unseen battles and quiet sacrifices. We have explored how God uses hardship to shape the heart of a pastor, how criticism often cuts deeper than gratitude, and how spiritual warfare presses hardest on those entrusted with leading His people. But as we gather these truths into one final understanding, this remains clear. You are never truly alone in this calling.

Pastor, leader, servant of God, hear this clearly. Your tears are not wasted. Your weariness is not ignored. Your sacrifices are not forgotten. Heaven keeps record of what earth often overlooks.

When you feel unseen, remember Hagar's cry in the wilderness, "You are the God who sees me" (Genesis 16:13). When you feel inadequate, remember Paul's thorn and the Lord's reply, "My grace is sufficient for you, for My strength is made perfect in weakness" (2 Corinthians 12:9). When you feel abandoned, remember the promise of Jesus Himself, "Lo, I am with you always, even unto the end of the world" (Matthew 28:20).

Leadership is lonely, but it is also holy. The Shepherd who called you has not left you to carry the rod and the staff alone. He walks with you. He upholds you. He whispers strength into your spirit when no one else hears the struggle.

As you close this book, do not allow its truths to remain on these pages. Live them. Carry them. Let them steady you. When affliction comes, do not shrink back, but recognize the refining hand of God. When criticism cuts, do not let it define you, but measure your worth by obedience rather than applause. When warfare rages, do not faint, but stand firm, knowing the victory has already been secured. When loneliness presses in, do not despair, but lean fully into the presence of the Chief Shepherd, for His nearness is enough.

This is not theory. This is survival. This is ministry. This is Kingdom work.

And when weariness returns, as it surely will, come back to these truths and allow them to breathe fresh courage into your spirit.

Here is the wisdom that must remain with you. The burden you carry is proof of the trust God has placed upon your life. If this calling were easy, anyone could do it. But He chose you. And if He called you, He will also keep you.

So stand. Preach when your heart feels heavy. Pray when your knees feel weak. Love when your spirit feels emptied. The Shepherd who called you is the same Shepherd who sustains you.

One day, when the sermons are finished, the prayers are prayed, and the battles are complete, you will hear the only words that truly matter:

"Well done, good and faithful servant."

Until that day, keep walking. Keep leading. Keep leaning on the One who never leaves you.

Until you are the pastor, you cannot fully understand these realities. But if you are the pastor, take courage. God Himself shepherds you even as you shepherd others.

We close not with a period, but with a prayer.

A Prayer of Commissioning

Father in Heaven,

We lift before You every shepherd who carries Your name and every servant who bears the weight of Your people. You see their tears, their unseen sacrifices, and their silent battles. You know the burdens they cannot speak aloud.

Strengthen them with a fresh wind of Your Spirit. Guard their hearts from bitterness, their minds from weariness, and their bodies from fainting. Let their skin be thick enough to endure criticism, yet their hearts remain soft with the compassion of Christ.

Clothe them in the armor of God when warfare rises. Whisper peace into their souls when loneliness presses in. Remind them daily that their worth is not found in the applause of people, but in the smile of Heaven.

Raise them as voices of truth in a culture of confusion, as lights on a hill that cannot be hidden, and as shepherds who reflect the heart of the Chief Shepherd, Jesus Christ.

And when their race is finished, may they stand before You and hear, "Well done, good and faithful servant." Until that day, keep them faithful. Keep them humble. Keep them close to Your heart.

In the mighty name of Jesus,

Amen.

Epilogue
A Final Word to the Pastor's Heart

Dear Shepherd,

If you have read these pages, know this for certain: you are not alone. Your struggles are not strange, your wounds are not wasted, and your tears are not unseen. The road of ministry may feel lonely at times, but it is never empty, for the same God who called you walks faithfully beside you.

Remember this truth. The sheep do not define the shepherd. The Shepherd defines the shepherd. Your worth is not measured by applause or attendance, but by Heaven's affirmation. When gratitude is scarce and criticism is loud, let His quiet whisper steady your heart.

You will not always see the full fruit of your labor in this lifetime. Some seeds you plant will be harvested by another generation. Yet the soil remembers. Heaven keeps record. And eternity will one day reveal what earth overlooked.

So preach again. Love again. Lead again. And when you feel as though you cannot take another step, rest in the arms of the One who neither slumbers nor sleeps.

Lift your eyes. You are not carrying this calling alone. The Chief Shepherd walks with you. And one day, when all is said and done, you will lay down the staff you carried and receive the crown He promised.

Until then, remain faithful. And remember this above all: being a pastor is not about being perfect. It is about being faithful to the One who is.

With you in the journey,

Pastor Stamford B. Jackson Sr.

"And when the Chief Shepherd appears, you will receive the unfading crown of glory."

— *1 Peter 5:4*

Acknowledgements

I would like to first acknowledge **the late Apostle K. L. Warren,** whose apostolic wisdom, leadership, and poise were poured into my life over the many years I had the privilege of serving under him. His voice, instruction, and example shaped my understanding of ministry in ways I continue to walk out today.

Sir, I now truly understand your words: *Until you're the Pastor, you're not.*

I also extend my sincere gratitude to **Pastor Charles McCarley** and **Apostle Arthur Hinton.** Thank you for your guidance, wisdom, steadfast support, and continual encouragement. Your investment in my life and calling has made a lasting impact, and I am deeply grateful.

About the Author
Pastor Stamford Jackson

Pastor Stamford B. Jackson Sr. was born and raised on the beautiful island of Bermuda, where the foundations of his faith were established within the New Testament Church of God. Growing up in a strong church community, he developed a deep love for worship, service, and the Word of God from an early age. In 2007, he accepted the call to ministry under the leadership of Apostle D. C. Grant and Senior Pastor M. D. Grant at New Genesis Embassy in Bermuda.

Throughout his years in ministry, Pastor Jackson has served with excellence and humility in various leadership roles, including Chief Armor Bearer and Associate Pastor. Each assignment has strengthened his passion for servant leadership and reinforced his belief that true greatness in the Kingdom of God is found in serving others. His ministry is rooted in the conviction that "to serve is to live," and he has devoted his life to mentoring, discipling, and equipping believers to walk boldly in their God-given destiny.

Pastor Jackson's vision is to see the body of Christ strengthened, minds renewed beyond worldly systems, and lives restored to God's original design. His leadership is marked by integrity, compassion, and a Kingdom-focused perspective that seeks to cultivate culture-shifting disciples and leaders for Christ.

Beyond the pulpit, Pastor Jackson treasures his role as a husband and father. He believes family is the first and most sacred ministry, and he carries that same love and devotion into every aspect of his Kingdom assignment. In his personal time, he is an entrepreneur who enjoys studying the Word of God, building meaningful relationships, and drawing inspiration from his favorite scripture: *"But seek ye first the kingdom of God, and his righteousness; and all these things shall be added unto you"* (Matthew 6:33).

His life's mission remains clear: to glorify God through faithful service and to see the will of God accomplished on earth as it is in heaven.

Stay Connected!

Stay connected and grow with us beyond these pages.

We invite you to visit **Kingdom Vision Center International Ministries** on Facebook, where you'll find prayer, live-streamed Sunday services, Bible studies, and ongoing encouragement for your faith journey. Whether you're seeking community, sound teaching, or a place to be refreshed in God's presence, you are welcome to join us!

https://www.facebook.com/kingdomvision1971

www.ingramcontent.com/pod-product-compliance
Lightning Source LLC
LaVergne TN
LVHW051815080426
835513LV00017B/1970